Fine Points for Legal Writing

Fine Points for Legal Writing

By Wayne Schiess

Other books by Wayne Schiess:

- *Legal Writing Nerd: Be One*
- *Writing for the Legal Audience*
- *Plain Legal Writing: Do It*
- *Advanced Legal Writing Workshop*

For Emmy, Cohen, Calvin, Cora, Brynn, and Etta.

Thank you, Ann Darrington.

Table of Contents

Fine Points for Legal Writing

Introduction

I've been teaching legal writing for a long time, and I've seen a certain group of mistakes a lot. I wrote this book to help law students avoid those mistakes and learn some of the key conventions of legal writing.

The book addresses the most-common mechanical writing mistakes law students make. "Mechanical" means grammar, punctuation, usage (how words are used), and style—the conventions of professional, written legal English. The book also covers a few types of citation errors and explains the conventions for quoting in legal writing. Finally, it describes some points of format and typography.

You should review these rules and learn to eliminate mistakes as you edit your legal writing. If your legal-writing professor refers you to an item in this book, look it up and study it. Eventually, you'll avoid making the mistakes in the first place.

Why this emphasis on mechanics? Lawyers tend to be fussy about mechanics. They want things right—perfect. They often view mechanical mistakes as suggesting that you're not smart or that you're lazy. Both are bad. To please your audience in the legal writing you do, master these Fine Points.

Writing rules do sometimes change: words change, grammar changes, and punctuation changes, too. In standard written English in the United States, these changes can sometimes happen quickly. But in legal writing, change happens slowly or not at all. For several of the rules in this book, legal writing has not caught up with the changes in other forms of writing. When that's true, the rule will say so.

By the way—this book is not comprehensive. It contains only the most-common mistakes and stylistic problems I've seen over the years. If you want a comprehensive legal-writing reference, ask your legal-writing professor for a recommendation.

In my view, law is a writing profession, and lawyers are professional writers. I hope this books helps you become one.

-Wayne Schiess

Definitions

1. Clause

A group of words with a subject and a verb. It may be dependent or independent.

2. Conjunctive adverb (transition word)

A traditional transition word that is longer than a coordinating conjunction: *furthermore, however, therefore.* See 14.

3. Coordinating conjunction

Short words that connect things: *and, but, for, nor, or, yet, so.*

4. Dependent clause

A group of words with a subject and verb but that is not a complete thought. It could not be a sentence by itself. Typically it lacks an object or begins with a subordinating adverb. See 9.

5. Independent clause
A group of words with a subject and verb and that is a complete thought. It could be a sentence by itself.

6. Phrase
A group of words that is not a clause of either kind because it has no subject, no verb, or neither.

7. Pronoun agreement
To agree, a pronoun must agree with (match) its antecedent, the original noun it refers to, in number and gender.

8. Run-on sentence
Improperly joined independent clauses. When independent clauses are joined without punctuation, without a coordinating conjunction, or with only a comma (a comma splice), that is a run-on sentence. It does not mean a long sentence.

9. Subordinating adverb
Words that begin dependent clauses and render them dependent, as opposed to independent. Many relate to time, for example: *after, before, since, until, when, whenever, while.* Others suggest cause or other relationships: *although, because, despite, if, though, unless, whereas, whether.*

Grammar & Punctuation

10. Apostrophe for possessive, singular but not ending in *s*

Form *singular* possessives by adding *apostrophe + s*.

- the court's authority
- Pam's house

Do not use an apostrophe for plurals or possessive pronouns.

10a.**Wrong**: send it to both office's
10b. send it to both offices

10c.**Wrong**: the company fired it's employee
10d. the company fired its employee

11. Apostrophe for possessive, plural

Form *plural* possessives ending in *s* or *es* by adding only an apostrophe.

- the Schiesses' house
- her two bosses' cars

12. Apostrophe for possessive, singular and ending in *s*
Form singular possessives of words ending in *s* by adding *apostrophe* + *s* (traditional convention) or by adding just an apostrophe (journalism convention).

12a. **Preferred**: her boss's car
12b. **Preferred**: Texas's boundaries

or

12c. her boss' car
12d. Texas' boundaries

13. Beginning sentences—no numerals or symbols
Don't begin a sentence with a symbol (§) or a numeral (2018).

13a. **Wrong**: § 216(b) allows punitive damages
13b. Section 216(b) allows punitive damages.
13c. **Wrong**: 2019 was the year Key Co. acquired Setcom.
13d. Key Co. acquired Setcom in 2019.

14. Comma after introductory transition word (conjunctive adverb); see 2
Place a comma after an introductory transition word (also called a conjunctive adverb). Common conjunctive adverbs:

accordingly	nevertheless
consequently	nonetheless
finally	otherwise
furthermore	similarly
however	still
likewise	subsequently
meanwhile	therefore
moreover	thus

14a. Similarly, Rei does not object to the fee amount.

14b. However, Rei asks that the amount not be disclosed to the public.

14c. Lin wrote the brief in one day; therefore, she did not have time to polish it.

15. Comma after introductory clause or long phrase

Place a comma after an introductory clause. A comma after a short introductory phrase is optional.

15a. Although the transaction closed on time, the client was still unhappy.

15b. If clients are seeking emotional satisfaction, a lawsuit is not the right solution.

15c. In *Megha v. Lender Center, Inc.*, the court issued a 90-page opinion.

15d. **Optional**: In 2004, Joanne enrolled in law school.

16. Comma before coordinating conjunction in a series—two options; see 3

Preferred: Place a comma before the coordinating conjunction in a series—the best practice for legal writing. Conjunctions: *and, or, for, nor, but, yet,* and *so*. Whatever convention you use, be consistent.

16a. **Preferred**: The flag is red, white, and blue.

16b. **Preferred**: The prosecutor filed charges of second-degree murder, manslaughter, and unlawful practice of medicine against Gonzalez's widow.

Other option: Some lawyers and many journalists omit the comma before the conjunction.

16c. **Acceptable**: The flag is red, white and blue.

16d. **Acceptable**: The prosecutor filed charges of second-degree murder, manslaughter and unlawful practice of medicine against Gonzalez's widow.

17. Comma between independent clauses joined by a coordinating conjunction; see 3, 5

Place a comma before a conjunction that joins independent clauses. Conjunctions: *and, or, for, nor, but, yet,* and *so.*

> 17a. Terry went to the store, and she came home.
> 17b. Litigation practice can be exciting, but the workload can sometimes be heavy.

If what follows the conjunction is a phrase or dependent clause (could not be a sentence by itself) a comma is usually not needed.

> 17c. Terry went to the store and came home.
> 17d. Litigation practice can be exciting but also exhausting.

18. Commas for appositives

An appositive restates or renames a noun it follows. It requires two commas.

> 18a. **Wrong**: The defendant, Ms. Lang did not hire a lawyer.
> 18b. The defendant, Ms. Lang, did not hire a lawyer.

19. Commas for city, state

Place a comma after the city and the state in city-state format:

> 19a. **Wrong**: The appellant was born in Austin, Texas and left there in 1991.
> 19b. The appellant was born in Austin, Texas, and left there in 1991.

20. Commas for full date

Place a comma after the date and year in a full date in month-date-year format:

20a. **Wrong**: The closing occurred on May 2, 2018 at the buyer's offices.

20b. The closing occurred on May 2, 2018, at the buyer's offices.

21. Commas to set off nonrestrictive clauses; see 1

Use commas to set off nonrestrictive clauses—groups of words that have a subject and a verb and that add parenthetical or additional information about a topic. Omit the commas if the clause is restrictive—it defines or limits the topic.

21a. **Nonrestrictive clause**: The security guard, who was wearing sunglasses, pushed the plaintiff.

- There is one security guard and, by the way, that security guard was wearing sunglasses.

21b. **Restrictive clause**: The security guard who was wearing sunglasses pushed the plaintiff.

- There is more than one security guard, and the one who pushed the plaintiff was wearing sunglasses.

When the topic is not a person, the same rule applies, but the nonrestrictive clause begins with *which* and the restrictive clause begins with *that*.

21c. **Nonrestrictive**: The lawnmower, which is broken, is in the garage.

- There is one lawnmower and, by the way, it is broken.

21d. **Restrictive**: The lawnmower that is broken is in the garage.

- There is more than one lawnmower. The broken lawnmower is in the garage.

21e. **Nonrestrictive clause**: New water laws were needed in the western states, which relied on irrigation.

- All western states relied on irrigation.

21f. **Restrictive clause**: New water laws were needed in the western states that relied on irrigation.

- Only some western states relied on irrigation.

22. Commas to set off nonrestrictive participial (-*ing* verb) phrases

Use a comma or commas to set off a present participle (-*ing* verb) that introduces a nonrestrictive phrase. In other words, use a comma when the phrase applies to the earlier subject and not to the noun it follows.

22a. **Nonrestrictive phrase**: Auden addressed the judge, asserting that the Equitable Tolling doctrine applied. (*Auden is doing the asserting, not the judge.*)

22b. **Restrictive phrase**: Auden addressed the judge asserting that the Equitable Tolling doctrine applied. (*There is more than one judge, and Auden addressed the judge who was doing the asserting.*)

23. Hyphen for compound modifier (phrasal adjective)

Place a hyphen between words that jointly modify a noun.

- five-day period
- city-owned street
- board-appointed reviewer

The presence or absence of the hyphen can sometimes change the meaning:

23a. The state bar is offering a **new lawyer program**.

- This means a program for lawyers, and the program is new.

23b. The state bar is offering a **new-lawyer program**.

- This means a program for new lawyers

A multiple-word modifier requires multiple hyphens:
- all-or-nothing strategy
- on-the-spot investigation
- two-year-old plan

Don't hyphenate *-ly* adverbs, but do hyphenate phrases with *well*.
- highly respected judge
- well-known lawyer

Some legal writers avoid hyphenating standard legal phrases where no ambiguity will arise:
- summary judgment motion
- third party beneficiary
- good faith effort

Others consistently hyphenate compound modifiers to avoid having to assess the potential for ambiguity each time.

24. *That*, over-deleting

You may have been advised to delete the word *that* to streamline your sentences. It's fair advice, but it can go too far. Sometimes, deleting *that* causes a miscue for the reader.

24a. **Miscue:** The plaintiff argues the statute precludes all sovereign-immunity defenses.

- The miscue arises because the reader might initially assume that the plaintiff is arguing the statute—as opposed to arguing case law.

The sentence would be clearer with *that*:

24b. The plaintiff argues **that** the statute precludes all sovereign-immunity defenses.

24c. **Miscue**: A reasonable juror would be able to find Mason's errand was for the benefit of the employer.

- Reader's initial sense: "A reasonable juror would be able to find Mason's errand …." (Was it lost?)

The sentence would be clearer with *that*:

24d. A reasonable juror would be able to find **that** Mason's errand was for the benefit of the employer.

25. Modifier, dangling, and dangling participle

In a sentence with a dependent, introductory modifying phrase, that phrase or clause is deemed to modify the very next noun that follows it.

25a. **Wrong**: Speaking forcefully and passionately, the jury was swayed by defense attorney Juliet Anson as she made her closing argument.

- The introductory phrase is meant to modify *defense attorney Juliet Anson*, but it actually modifies *the jury*.

25b. Speaking forcefully and passionately, defense attorney Juliet Anson swayed the jury as she made her closing argument.

Sometimes the introductory phrase is meant to modify a noun that is missing from the sentence:

25c. **Wrong**: Having passed the bar exam, the swearing-in ceremony is next.

- The introductory phrase is meant to modify someone who has passed the bar exam, but that someone (noun), is missing.

25d. Having passed the bar exam, you will attend the swearing-in ceremony next.

26. Parallel structure, faulty

Parallel structure or parallelism means that when you write a series of items, phrases, or clauses, you must follow two rules:

- Each item, phrase, or clause in the series must flow naturally from the lead-in word.
- All items, phrases, and clauses in the series must begin with the same part of speech.

26a. When editing a legal document, students should look for spelling errors, scan for punctuation mistakes, and proofread the citations.

The lead-in word is *should*, and these are the phrases in a series:

- look for spelling errors
- scan for punctuation mistakes
- proofread the citations

All three phrases in the series fit naturally with the lead-in word, and all three begin with the same part of speech—**verbs**:

- should ... **look** for spelling errors
- ... **scan** for punctuation mistakes
- ... **proofread** the citations

26b. **Wrong**: When editing a legal document, students should look for spelling errors, punctuation mistakes, and proofread the citations.

Example 26b is faulty parallelism. The three phrases in the series do not all fit the lead-in word, and all three do not begin with the same part of speech:

- should ... **look** for spelling errors
- ... punctuation mistakes
- ... **proofread** the citations

27. Pronouns, first person and second person

Avoid first-person singular (*I*, *me*), first-person plural (*we*, *us*), and second-person pronouns (*you*) in formal documents such as memos, pleadings, and briefs. First- and second-person pronouns are appropriate in correspondence and informal documents.

28. Pronouns for courts and companies—singular; see 7

Treat courts and companies as singular.

28a. **Wrong**: The court has the authority to reverse their prior decision.

28b. The court has the authority to reverse its prior decision.

28c. **Wrong**: The company can rehire their former employees.

28d. The company can rehire its former employees.

29. Pronoun, singular use of plural pronoun *they*; see 7

The writing rules for what is called the "singular *they*" are changing. In legal writing, your professor or work supervisor may still consider it an error to refer to a singular noun (*employee*) with a plural pronoun (*they*) because pronouns should agree in number with their antecedents.

29a. **Nonstandard**: When an employee can prove a disability, **they** can receive benefits.

To avoid pronoun disagreement, some writers follow tradition and use male pronouns, which may be considered sexist.

29b. When an employee can prove a disability, **he** can receive benefits.

Some writers choose to use female pronouns.

29c. When an employee can prove a disability, **she** can receive benefits.

When writing for your professor or supervisor, it is often better to use *he or she*, or to write around the problem in some other way (plural, repetition):

29d. When an employee can prove a disability, he or she can receive benefits.

29e. When employees can prove a disability, they can receive benefits.

29f. When an employee can prove a disability, that employee can receive benefits.

Note: When writing about someone who has a preferred pronoun, follow that person's preference regardless of pronoun agreement.

30. Quotation marks, double for quotations; single for quoting within a quotation

This rule is changing in other forms of writing. But in legal writing, use double quotation marks for quotations and single for quoting within a quotation.

30a. **Wrong**: Jacobs got custody because he was considered a 'stable' parent.

30b. Mr. Jacobs got custody because he was considered a "stable" parent.

30c. Mr. Jacobs got custody because "he was considered a 'stable' parent."

31. Quotation marks, commas and periods inside

This rule is changing in other forms of writing. But in legal writing, place commas and periods inside quotation marks.

31a. **Nonstandard**: Mr. Jacobs got custody because, as a parent, he was considered "stable".

31b. **Preferred**: Mr. Jacobs got custody because, as a parent, he was considered "stable."

31c. **Nonstandard**: Even though Mr. Jacobs was a "stable parent", he did not get custody.

31d. **Preferred**: Even though Mr. Jacobs was a "stable parent," he did not get custody.

32. Run-on sentence (comma splice); see 8

Do not join independent clauses with only a comma, without punctuation, or without a coordinating conjunction.

32a. **Wrong**: We understand that there must be rules many forms of writing have rules.

32b. **Wrong**: We understand that there must be rules, many forms of writing have rules.

To fix the run-on, use a period, a semicolon, or a conjunction:

32c. We understand that there must be rules. Many forms of writing have rules.

32d. We understand that there must be rules; many forms of writing have rules.

32e. We understand that there must be rules, and many forms of writing have rules.

33. Run-on sentence, conjunctive adverb; see 2, 8

Do not join independent clauses with a conjunctive adverb and a comma. If the conjunctive adverb separates independent clauses, commas are insufficient.

33a. **Wrong:** Rei does not object to the fees, however, she asks that the amount not be disclosed to the public.

This is a form of run-on sentence or comma splice. To fix it, replace the first comma with a period and start a new sentence or replace the first comma with a semicolon.

33b. Rei does not object to the fees. However, she asks that the amount not be disclosed to the public.

33c. Rei does not object to the fees; however, she asks that the amount not be disclosed to the public.

This rule does not apply to coordinating conjunctions (like *but*).

33d. Rei does not object to the fees, but she asks that the amount not be disclosed to the public.

Below, 33e is correct because *however* doesn't separate independent clauses:

33e. Rei does not object to the fees. She asks, however, that the amount not be disclosed to the public.

34. Semicolon

A semicolon can separate independent clauses.

34a. Rei does not object to the amount of the fees; she asks that the amount not be disclosed to the public.

Semicolons separate phrases in a series when one or more of the phrases has internal commas.

34b. A client letter should begin with an up-front summary; follow that with the facts, the authority, and the analysis; and conclude with recommendations.

Semicolons can separate the items in a numbered list (commas are often also correct).

34c. When arguing a case to a jury, remember three things: (1) maintain regular but not constant eye contact; (2) keep your argument relatively short; and (3) close with a challenge.

34d. When arguing a case to a jury, remember three things:
(1) maintain regular but not constant eye contact;
(2) keep your argument relatively short; and
(3) close with a challenge.

Semicolons separate the authorities in a string citation.

34e. *Avant, Inc. v. Palmer*, 343 S.W.2d 282, 285 (Tex. 1983); *Cape v. Sanchez,* 201 S.W.2d 517, 522 (Tex. 1980).

Quoting

35. Quoting a passage

When: The quoted text is more than a word or phrase but is 49 words or fewer. *Bluebook* 5.1(b)

Place quotation marks before and after the quoted text. Cite the source immediately after the quotation.

35a. The Austin Court of Appeals stated, "A prevailing party on a claim for breach of fiduciary duty generally cannot recover attorney's fees." *Nikel v. Lamb*, 463 S.W.3d 200, 209 (Tex. App.—Austin 2015, no pet.)

36. Quoting a word or phrase

When: Quoting a key word or phrase that should be quoted on first use but not afterward (no ellipsis dots needed). *Bluebook* 5.1(b)(ii)

Place quotation marks around the quoted text. Cite the source immediately after the quotation or after the sentence in which the quotation appears.

36a. The Austin Court of Appeals held that the winner of a breach-of-fiduciary-duty lawsuit "generally cannot recover" the attorney's fees it incurred. *Nikel v.*

> *Lamb*, 463 S.W.3d 200, 209 (Tex. App.—Austin 2015, no pet.)

37. Block quotation

When: Quoting a passage of 50 words or more. *Bluebook* 5.1(a)

Place the quoted text in its own paragraph, without quotation marks; indent one tab length left and right. Cite the source on the next regular line of text. In double-spaced text, single-space the block.

37a. The Austin Court of Appeals held as follows:

> A prevailing party on a claim for breach of fiduciary duty generally cannot recover attorney's fees. The general rule in Texas is that, unless provided for by statute or contract, attorney's fees are not recoverable. But a court may award attorney's fees to a plaintiff in a shareholder suit if a substantial benefit to the corporation resulted.

> *Nikel v. Lamb*, 463 S.W.3d 200, 209 (Tex. App.— Austin 2015, no pet.)

38. Paraphrasing

When: The original language isn't crucial, but you want to convey its content.

Convey the original meaning with your own sentence structure and words, and cite the source immediately after.

38a. The Austin Court of Appeals has held that for breach of fiduciary duty, the party prevailing at trial cannot necessarily recover attorney's fees. *Nikel v. Lamb*,

463 S.W.3d 200, 209 (Tex. App.—Austin 2015, no pet.)

39. Altering

When: Altering text, changing case, or adding letters or words in quoted text. *Bluebook* 5.2

Place brackets around altered or added letters and words.

39a. The Austin Court of Appeals held that "[a] prevailing party on a claim for breach of fiduciary duty generally cannot recover attorney's fees [from its opponent]." *Nikel v. Lamb*, 463 S.W.3d 200, 209 (Tex. App.—Austin 2015, no pet.)

40. Omitting from the middle

When: Omitting from the middle of a quoted sentence. (No ellipsis dots for omissions at the beginning of a sentence.) *Bluebook* 5.3(b)(ii)

Place 3 ellipsis dots with 4 spaces [s] at the point of omission: [s].[s].[s].[s]

40a. The Austin Court of Appeals stated, "A prevailing party on a claim for breach of fiduciary duty . . . cannot recover attorney's fees. *Nikel v. Lamb*, 463 S.W.3d 200, 209 (Tex. App.—Austin 2015, no pet.)

41. Omitting from the end

When: Omitting from the end of a quoted sentence (even if the quotation continues). *Bluebook* 5.3(b)(iii)

Place 3 ellipsis dots with 4 spaces and then a period with a space at the point of omission: [s].[s].[s].[s]period[s]

41a. Referring to attorney's fees, the Austin Court of Appeals stated, "A prevailing party on a claim for breach of fiduciary duty generally cannot recover . . . ." *Nikel v. Lamb*, 463 S.W.3d 200, 209 (Tex. App.— Austin 2015, no pet.)

42. Omitting from the beginning

When: Omitting from the beginning of a quoted sentence after a quoted sentence. *Bluebook* 5.3(b)(v)

Place a period and then 3 ellipsis dots with 4 spaces at the point of omission: period[s].[s].[s].[s] Apply brackets as needed.

42a. The Austin Court of Appeals stated, "A prevailing party on a claim for breach of fiduciary duty generally cannot recover attorney's fees. . . . [U]nless provided for by statute or contract, attorney's fees are not recoverable. *Nikel v. Lamb*, 463 S.W.3d 200, 209 (Tex. App.—Austin 2015, no pet.)

Do not use ellipsis dots to indicate an omission at the opening of your quotation.

43. Omitting from end and beginning

When: Omitting from the end of a quoted sentence and continuing by omitting from the beginning of another quoted sentence. *Bluebook* 5.3(b)(vi)

Place 3 ellipsis dots with 4 spaces and then a period with a space at the point of omission: [s].[s].[s].[s]period[s]

43a. Referring to attorney's fees, the Austin Court of Appeals stated, "A prevailing party on a claim for breach of fiduciary duty generally cannot recover . . . . unless provided for by statute or contract . . . ." *Nikel v. Lamb*, 463 S.W.3d 200, 209 (Tex. App.—Austin 2015, no pet.)

Usage (Words)

44. *Argue*, courts don't

When writing about judicial opinions, avoid writing that courts

- argue
- assert
- maintain
- contend

Also avoid writing that courts

- think
- believe
- feel

Instead, use these words, as appropriate. Courts

- state
- opine
- decide
- conclude

Or use these other words: *find* (see 46), *hold* (see 47), *rule* (see 51).

45. Contractions

Avoid contractions in formal documents such as memos, pleadings, briefs, and transactional documents. Contractions are appropriate in correspondence and informal documents.

46. *Find*

Use *find* and *found* for the factual findings of a court (usually a trial court) and for decisions reached by a jury.

46a. The court found that the defendant was traveling 65 miles per hour.

46b. The jury found that the defendant was responsible for the injuries.

46c. **Wrong**: The appellate court found that the statute was unconstitutional.

47. *Hold*

Use *hold* and *held* for legal decisions and conclusions (by a trial or appellate court). In general, appellate courts *hold* (or *conclude, decide, state*) but rarely *find*.

47a. The Texas Supreme Court held the statute unconstitutional.

47b. The trial court held that driving a car after a diagnosis of narcolepsy was negligent as a matter of law.

48. *Instant case*, case at bar, case *sub judice*

It is not necessary to refer to the case you are analyzing or discussing as *the instant case*, the *case at bar*, or the *case sub judice*. Some professors and lawyers also object to *the case at bar*, although some are fine with all these phrases.

Generally, try to use *this case* (when not ambiguous) or *here*.

49. *Judgment,* not *judgement*

In the United States, lawyers spell this word *judgment.* Microsoft Word accepts *judgement* with an extra *e* in the middle, so use care.

50. *Motion, move*

When a party files a motion in court, the verb form is *move.*

  50a.**Wrong**: The defendant motioned for summary judgment.

  50b.The defendant moved for summary judgment.

51. *Rule*

Generally, when a court rules, it is a procedural action or a decision about evidence. Appellate courts usually don't rule.

52. *Said, herein, aforementioned,* and other archaisms

Avoid *said* if you could use *the* or another pronoun.

  52a.**Archaic**: Ms. Kenko signed the contract willingly but later alleged that she had signed said contract under duress.

  52b.Ms. Kenko signed the contract willingly but later alleged that she had signed the contract under duress.

Avoid *herein, aforementioned, thereto, wherein,* and the like.

  52c. **Archaic**: The cases cited herein do not support the aforementioned legal rules.

  52d.The cases cited here [in this memo] do not support the legal rules stated above.

53. Spelling

Do not rely only on spell check. Proofread carefully. Commonly misspelled words in legal writing are—

- *form* for *from*
- *libel* for *liable*
- *sing* for *sign*
- *statue* for *statute*
- *trail* for *trial*

54. *Testimony*, not *testimonies*

The word *testimony* is a "non-count noun," also called a "mass noun," which means that it does not take the standard "s" plural. When referring to the testimony of more than one person, use the word *testimony*, not *testimonies*.

54a. The jury believed testimony of both witnesses.
54b. Both witnesses' testimony was credible.

Others non-count or mass nouns that do not form a standard plural:

- *advice*
- *evidence*
- *information*
- *knowledge*
- *music*
- *software*

Citation

55. *Id.* always takes a period; mid-sentence *id.* is lowercase

Id. is an abbreviation of *idem*. When placed within a textual sentence, it is lowercase: *id*.

56. Citations, short forms for cases

Under the *Bluebook*, a short-form case citation, unless using *id.*, requires a single party name, the volume number, the reporter abbreviation, the word *at*, and the pinpoint page:

56a. *Centex*, 343 S.W.3d at 283.

So all the following are incorrect:

56b. **Wrong**: *Centex*, at 283.
56c. **Wrong**: *Centex*, 343 S.W.3d 283.
56d. **Wrong**: *Centex*, 343 S.W.3d 282, at 283.
56e. **Wrong**: *Centex v. Slack*, 343 S.W.3d at 282.

57. Citations, choosing shortened case names

When shortening a case name for a short-form citation, generally follow these guidelines:

- If the case is well known by a shortened name, use that name.
- Use the first party's name, unless an exception applies.
- If the first party's name is long or complex, you may shorten it. It's fine to use a two- or sometimes three-word name. You may drop Inc., Co., and the like.
- If the first party's name is long or complex and can't be easily shortened, you may use the second party's name.
- If the first party name is a governmental entity or person (United States, State, Commissioner, Secretary), or if it's a common litigant, use the second party's name.

58. Italics for case names

Use *italics*, not <u>underlining</u>, for case names in full-form and short-form citations. Italicize case names in shorthand references, too:

58a. the *Centex* case

59. Italics for signals

Italicize all *Bluebook* signals.

- *See*
- *See also*
- *See, e.g.,*

Italicizing or not italicizing the punctuation can be tricky, so check with your professor or supervisor about how picky you should be.

60. Spacing abbreviations

Close up single adjacent single capital letters and numeric ordinals; put a space between multi-letter abbreviations.

60a.**Wrong**: S. D. N. Y., S. W. 3d
60b. S.D.N.Y., S.W.3d
60c. **Wrong**: Tex.App., F.Supp.2d
60d. Tex. App., F. Supp. 2d

Writing "Rules" That Aren't

61. *And*, beginning with

Some professors and lawyers enforce a rule against beginning a sentence with *and*. There is no such rule. Beginning with *and* might be considered informal, so if you're writing for a professor or lawyer who follows this rule, you might have to follow it. When beginning with *and*, you need no comma.

62. *But*, beginning with

Some professors and lawyers enforce a rule against beginning a sentence with *but*. There is no such rule. If you're writing for a professor or lawyer who follows the rule, you might have to follow it. But the United States Constitution has seven sentences beginning with *but*. When beginning with *but*, you need no comma.

63. *However*, beginning with

Some professors and lawyers enforce a rule against beginning a sentence with *however*. There is no such rule. It's a stylistic preference. However, if you're writing for a professor or lawyer who follows the rule, you might have to follow it. When beginning with *however*, you do need a comma.

64. Infinitives, splitting

Some professors and lawyers enforce a rule against splitting an infinitive. An infinitive is the word *to* plus a base verb:

- to read
- to write
- to edit

If you follow the rule against splitting infinitives, you do not insert an adverb between *to* and the base verb. So these would be wrong:

- to thoroughly read
- to quickly write
- to carefully edit

There is no such rule. It's a misguided stylistic preference, but if you're writing for a professor or lawyer who follows the rule, you might have to reluctantly follow it.

65. Preposition, ending with

Some professors and lawyers enforce a rule against ending a sentence, or even a clause within a sentence, with a preposition. Under this rule, these would be wrong:

65a. The defendant named three witnesses whom the prosecutor had never heard of.

65b. The building at 301 Cannon Road is not the building that the chief financial officer was referring to.

There is no such rule. Ending with a preposition might be considered informal, so if you're writing for a professor or lawyer who follows the rule, you might have to follow it, too.

To avoid ending with a preposition, try to revise in a way that avoids awkward work-arounds:

65c. **Poor**: The defendant named three witnesses of whom the prosecutor had never heard.

65d. **Better**: The prosecutor had never heard of the three witnesses the defendant named.

65e. **Better**: The defendant named three witnesses, but the prosecutor had never heard of them.

65f. **Poor**: The building at 301 Cannon Road is not the building to which the chief financial officer was referring.

65g. **Better**: The chief financial officer was not referring to the building at 301 Cannon Road.

65h. **Better**: The chief financial officer was referring to a building, but it was not the building at 301 Cannon Road.

Format & Typography

66. Dash or em dash

For emphasis and in Texas Courts of Appeals citations, use the full-length em dash (—), not the shorter en dash (–). Omitting spaces around two hyphens should cause Microsoft Word to auto-correct to the proper dash. Using spaces will produce the shorter, incorrect dash.

66a. **Wrong**: The client – not the lawyer – must make the decision.

66b. The client—not the lawyer—must make the decision.

66c. **Wrong**: *Cape v. Sanchez,* 925 S.W.2d 517, 522 (Tex. App. – Austin 1995, no writ).

66d. *Cape v. Sanchez,* 925 S.W.2d 517, 522 (Tex. App.— Austin 1995, no writ).

67. En dash

The en dash (–) is shorter than the dash or em dash (—) and is used to separate numbers in year and page spans:

67a. 2018–19

67b. 343–44

Some professors and lawyers prefer or allow a hyphen in place of an en dash, so check with your professor or supervisor.

    67c. 2018-19
    67d. 343-44

68. Ellipsis

The *Bluebook* uses spaces and periods for an ellipsis, not the ellipsis symbol. Check Microsoft Word's auto-correct options to control this.

    68a. **Ellipsis symbol**: This is the way ... to write a brief.
    68b. **Periods and spaces**: This is the way . . . to write a brief.

69. Headings

In legal writing, headings can be emphasized with **boldface**, ***bold italics***, or *italics*. Although it is outdated to use underlining and ALL-CAPITALS for headings, your professor or supervisor may prefer those formats.

The heading should be closer to the text below it than to the text above it or, at least, equally distant from the text above and below.

Legal writing generally uses two types of headings. Topic headings are a single word or a short phrase and use Initial Capitals (capitalize all words except conjunctions, articles, and prepositions) without a period:

    69a. **Argument, Discussion, Statement of Facts, Conclusion**

Point headings are complete sentences. They use sentence case (capitalize the first word) and take a period:

    69b. **Dayson Company can raise a fact question as to the alleged oral warning.**

    69c. **The trial court erred in concluding that, as a matter of law, Dayson Company provided an oral warning.**

70. Hyphen

The hyphen (-) connects prefixes, joins compound-modifying words (see 23), and may be used for number spans.

    70a. pre-1990, quasi-contract
    70b. legal-writing professor, three-page memo
    70c. 2018-19, 343-44

71. Italics, not underlining

In legal writing, modern practice is to *italicize* and avoid underlining.

72. Justification

The body text of legal documents can be justified (also *fully justified*) or left justified (also *left aligned*). Check with your professor or supervisor and match that person's preference.

Fully justified text looks like this. Fully justified text looks like this. Fully justified text looks like this. Fully justified text looks like this. Fully justified text looks like this. Meanwhile, fully justified text looks like this.

Left-justified text looks like this. Left-justified text looks like this. Left-justified text looks like this. Left-justified text looks like this. Left-justified text looks like this. Meanwhile, left-justified text looks like this.

73. Line spacing—single or double

Many legal documents, especially courts documents and memos, are double spaced, and many lawyers prefer double spacing. Letters and e-mail are single spaced (or spaced at 1.1 to 1.2).

Single line spacing looks like this. Single spacing looks like this, and single spacing looks like this. Single spacing looks like this, but single spacing looks like this. Single spacing looks like this. Meanwhile, single spacing looks like this. Single spacing looks like this.

Double spacing looks like this. Double spacing looks like

this. Double spacing looks like this. Double spacing looks like

this. Double spacing looks like this. Double spacing looks like

this. Double spacing looks like this. Double spacing looks like

this. Meanwhile, double spacing looks like this.

74. Margins

Most legal documents have 1-inch margins at the top, bottom, left, and right. You may use larger left-right margins—they make the document less crowded—but don't make your margins smaller than 1 inch. Try 1.3 to 1.5 inches.

75. Numerals—two options

Match your professor's or supervisor's preference for numerals in legal writing:

Option 1: Spell out numbers one to ten and use numerals for 11 and higher.

Option 2: The *Bluebook* requires, and many lawyers prefer, spelling out zero to ninety-nine and using numerals for 100 and higher.

76. Paragraphs—tab style or block style

Court documents and legal memos typically use tab style: indent the first line of each paragraph. Letters and e-mail typically use block style: do not indent the first line, but add extra space between paragraphs.

> Tab style looks like this. Tab style looks like this. Tab style looks like this. Tab style looks like this. Tab style looks like this. Tab style looks like this. Tab style looks like this. Tab style looks like this.
>
> Tab style looks like this. Tab style looks like this. Tab style looks like this. Tab style looks like this. Tab style looks like this. Tab style looks like this. Tab style looks like this.

> Block style looks like this. Block style looks like this. Block style looks like this. Block style looks like this. Block style looks like this. Block style looks like this.
>
> Block style looks like this. Block style looks like this. Block style looks like this. Block style looks like this. Block style looks like this. Block style looks like this.

77. Quotation marks, curved, not straight

Use curved (smart) quotation marks instead of "straight quotes." Straight quotes are for feet and inches: 5' 11".

- Not these: "no"
- But these: "yes"

Change the default setting so you'll always get the proper, curved quotation marks. These instructions are for Microsoft Word on a PC:

> Go to File > Options > Proofing > AutoCorrect Options and click on the tab for AutoFormat As You Type. Under "Replace as you type," check the box for "Straight quotes" with "smart quotes."

78. Section symbol (§) with non-breaking (hard) space

To insert the section symbol, you may use the function Insert > Symbol and then select the section symbol. Use a hard space (control + shift + space) after the section symbol.

79. Spaces after periods—two options

Match your professor's or supervisor's preference for spaces after periods and be consistent.

Option 1: Use one space after periods. This is the modern convention in professional writing, but it is not yet universal in legal writing.

Option 2: Use two spaces after periods. Some lawyers prefer two spaces.

80. Superscript ordinals—not in legal writing

In legal writing and in legal citations, use non-superscript ordinals.

80a. **Wrong**: 5th Cir., 1st Dist.
80b. 5th Cir., 1st Dist.

Microsoft Word will automatically make ordinals superscript. Take these steps to stop it.

Go to Options > Proofing > AutoCorrect Options and click on the tab called AutoFormat As You Type. Uncheck "Ordinals (1st) with superscript."

Go to Options > Proofing > AutoCorrect Options and click on the tab called AutoFormat. Uncheck "Ordinals (1st) with superscript."

81. Typefaces and fonts

In general, the body text and headings in your document should be in a serifed font, like Century Schoolbook, used here. (Others are Book Antiqua, Cambria, Garamond). It is acceptable to use boldface sans serif fonts like Calibri (others are Corbel, Franklin, Verdana) for short, topic headings, as this book does.

Full-sentence point headings should use the same font as the body text and be emphasized with bold or *italics*. See 69.

Index

Made in the USA
Columbia, SC
07 September 2021